THE LIBRARY OF
WOLVES AND WILD DOGS

THE GRAY WOLF

Fred H. Harrington

The Rosen Publishing Group's

PowerKids Press™
New York

*To the gray wolf of the Harris Lake pack we called 2407. She and her pack taught me
a lot about wolves. Although she has long since moved on, I will never forget her haunting eyes.*

Published in 2002 by The Rosen Publishing Group, Inc.
29 East 21st Street, New York, NY 10010

First Edition

Book Design: Michael de Guzman

Project Editor: Emily Raabe

Photo Credits: p. 4 © Lynn M. Stone (digital manipulation by Michael de Guzman); pp. 8, 11, 15, 22 © Lynn M. Stone; p. 6 (Chihuahua) © Mitchell Gerber/CORBIS; p. 6 (Saint Bernard) © Yann Arthus-Bertrand/CORBIS; pp. 7, 21 © Layne Kennedy/ CORBIS; p. 12 © Don Enger/Animals Animals; p. 16 © Peter Weimann/Animals Animals; p. 19 © Victoria McCormick/Animals Animals.

Harrington, Fred H.
     The gray wolf / by Fred H. Harrington.—1st ed.
          p. cm. — (The library of wolves and wild dogs)
     ISBN 0–8239–5764–0
     1. Wolves—Juvenile literature. [1. Wolves.] I. Title. II. Series.
     QL737.C22 H367 2002
     599.733—dc21

Manufactured in the United States of America

Contents

North
America

Europe

Asia

Kinds of Wolves

There are three kinds of wolves: gray wolves, red wolves, and Ethiopian wolves. Red wolves and Ethiopian wolves are very rare. Most of the wolves that live in North America, Europe, and Asia are gray wolves. Gray wolves also are called by other names, such as timber wolf or arctic wolf. These wolves are really just gray wolves that have **adapted** to different kinds of **habitats**. A timber wolf, for example, lives in the forest. Its gray fur helps it blend into forest shadows. An arctic wolf lives on the open **tundra**. There are no trees where arctic wolves live, so their white fur helps them blend with the snow. Even though they do not look like one another, the timber wolf and the arctic wolf are both gray wolves.

 Gray wolves were once found all over Europe, North America, and Asia. They lived everywhere except in deserts and very high mountain ranges.

Wolves and Dogs

Gray wolves are the largest members of the dog **family**. Adult wolves weigh from 80 to 120 pounds (36 to 54 kg), although one male wolf from Alaska weighed 175 pounds (79 kg)! The dog family includes wolves, foxes, domestic dogs such as collies and German shepherds, and wild dogs such as dingoes and African wild dogs. These animals are different from one another because they have adapted to different habitats and ways of life. Scientists put them in the same family,

Believe it or not, this furry Saint Bernard is a relative of the wolf!

Wolves were first tamed as pets about 20,000 years ago. All dogs, including this Chihuahua, come from these early tamed wolves.

though, because they are related to one another. Gray wolves are so closely related to red wolves and coyotes, in fact, that they can **mate** with them and have mixed-breed puppies. The closest of all the gray wolf's relatives is the domestic dog, from tiny Chihuahuas to great big Saint Bernards. Gray wolves and domestic dogs are still different animals, though. Gray wolves are adapted to living in the wild, and domestic dogs are adapted to living with people.

Unlike its dog relatives, the gray wolf is not adapted to living with humans.

Wolves Have to Eat

Gray wolves are **predators**, which means that they eat other animals. The animals that gray wolves eat are called **prey**. These prey animals have one thing in common.
They are big!

In North America, gray wolves eat large animals, such as deer, moose, elk, and caribou. Because these animals are big and strong, they are **dangerous** to hunt. Wolves can get injured or even killed by these prey animals, if they are not careful. To capture these large prey animals, gray wolves hunt in groups, called packs. Most packs have from 4 to 10 members, but some can have more than 30. Even so, most prey can escape from wolf packs. Usually, only sick, old, or just plain unlucky animals get caught and eaten by wolves.

 This wolf pack is feeding on their kill.

Wolf Families

Most people know that gray wolves live in packs, but many people really don't know what a pack is. Some people think a pack is just a bunch of wolves that get together, like a pack of neighborhood dogs. A gray wolf pack is different from a pack of dogs. It is a family of wolves, just like a family of people. Wolf packs have two parents and their children of different ages. The big difference between wolves and humans is that wolves have their babies every year in batches, called **litters**. Each litter has from four to seven puppies. Sometimes wolves might have as many as 11 puppies in the same litter!

These puppies are begging for food by licking the adult wolf's mouth. If the adult wolf has food in its stomach, it will throw up some for the hungry puppies to eat.

Living in a Den

Wolf puppies are born in a den. Having a den gives the pack a safe place to keep its puppies when they are very young. Mother wolves begin to build their dens at least three weeks before their pups are born. Other members of the pack often will help the mother to build her den. Wolves usually dig their dens in sandy ground or under big rocks. Sometimes they borrow dens from other animals, such as foxes. A pack might use a different den each year, or it might use the same den for many years. One famous den on Ellesmere Island in northern Canada probably has been used by arctic wolves for more than 700 years!

These curious wolf puppies will use their den for eight to ten weeks. After that, they will begin to explore more widely with the other members of their pack.

Growing up in a Pack

Gray wolf puppies are born in the spring. When they are born, they weigh less than a pound (.5 kg), but they grow quickly. The puppies' older brothers and sisters help raise them by babysitting the puppies while their parents are hunting. Sometimes the older brothers and sisters help their parents hunt. Being helpers at the den teaches these older brothers and sisters to be good parents. If the older wolves are good hunters, the pups might weigh 70 pounds (32 kg) by the time they are six months old! By then, they are almost as big as their parents. At

Puppies usually stay with the pack until·they are two or three years old. At that age, they will leave to make their own packs.

this point, the puppies no longer live in the den. They travel with the pack. By traveling with their pack, the puppies learn to hunt. This is also how the puppies learn about their pack's **territory**.

Wolves howl to communicate with other members of the pack. If pack members get lost, they can listen for their wolf pack's howl to find their way home.

Howling at Strangers

Each wolf pack lives in its own area, called a territory. A pack chases away any strange wolves it finds in its territory. This can be dangerous because wolves sometimes are injured or killed while trying to protect their territory. Guarding the territory is important because it keeps other wolves from eating the pack's prey. It also gives the puppies in the pack a safe place to grow up.

Before wolves go on a hunt, they often get together as a group and howl. Other wolves many miles away can hear the pack howl. This lets the other wolves know where the pack is. The other wolves can avoid fighting by staying away from the pack that is howling.

17

Smelling Is Believing

Wolves use scent marking to protect their territory and to avoid fighting. When wolves urinate, they leave a scent that can last for weeks. Wolves spend a lot of time sniffing scent marks because they can learn a lot about the wolf that left them. They can learn whether the wolf was a member of their pack or if it was a stranger. They also can learn whether it was a male or a female, if it was sick or well, and when it left the scent mark. By leaving scent marks, wolves keep strangers out of their territory. By sniffing scent marks, wolves can travel more safely. They can avoid their enemies and they can find their friends.

Wolves often leave scent marks on bushes, logs, tree trunks, or rocks.

When People Fear Wolves

Gray wolves once lived nearly everywhere in North America, Europe, and Asia. People thought the wolves were dangerous. They hated wolves because wolves sometimes killed sheep and cows. People killed wolves whenever they could. In some European countries, such as England, Ireland, and Holland, people killed all the wolves. Wolves **survived** in other countries, such as Italy and Spain, but only near forests where they could hide. In the United States, people **eliminated** wolves from almost all the states, except for Minnesota and Alaska. Today, however, many people realize that predators, such as the wolf, are important links in nature's food chain. If there are no predators, too many prey animals will survive. There will be more prey animals than there will be food for them, and

These gray wolves live in the state of Minnesota, one of the few places in the world where wolves are not seriously endangered.

many of them will die of starvation. Many people want to see the wolf return to places where it once lived.

When People Respect Wolves

Yellowstone National Park, in Wyoming, is famous for its natural wonders, such as its hot springs and geysers. Today it is also famous for its wolves. Gray wolves lived in Yellowstone when the park was started more than 100 years ago. Back then, people believed that wolves were bad because they killed other wildlife. All the wolves in Yellowstone were killed. Now we know that wolves help to keep prey, such as elk and deer, healthy and **alert.** In December 1994, scientists captured wolves in Canada. The scientists moved the wolves to Yellowstone and released them into the park three months later. These wolves quickly adapted to their new home. Now people can watch gray wolves hunt elk and **bison**, play with one another, and raise their pups.

Glossary

adapted (uh-DAPT-ed) To have changed to fit new conditions.

alert (uh-LERT) To be paying attention to what is around you.

bison (BI-sen) A large animal with a big head and a hump on its back.

dangerous (DAYN-jer-us) Something that can cause harm or injury.

eliminated (ih-LIH-muh-nay-ted) To have removed from; to have gotten rid of.

family (FAM-lee) The scientific name for a large group of plants or animals that are alike in some ways.

habitats (HA-bih-tats) The surroundings where an animal or a plant naturally lives.

litters (LIH-turz) A group of baby animals born to the same mother at the same time.

mate (MAYT) When a male and female join together to make babies.

predators (PREH-duh-terz) Animals that kill other animals for food.

prey (PRAY) An animal that is killed and eaten by other animals.

survived (sur-VYVD) Lived longer than; stayed alive.

territory (TEHR-uh-tohr-ee) Land or space protected by an animal for its use.

tundra (TUN-druh) The frozen land of the coldest parts of the world.

Index

Web Sites

To learn more about gray wolves, check out these Web sites:

www.wolf.org

www.wolfpark.org

www.yellowstone-natl-park.com/wolf.htm